Road *to* Routines

AMAAN MOTIWALA

INDIA · SINGAPORE · MALAYSIA

To Mom and Dad,
for their endless love,
support,
and encouragement.

Contents

Foreword

It is with immense pride and heartfelt admiration that I write this foreword for "Road to Routines." I have had the distinct pleasure of knowing this remarkable young man, Amaan, since he was just a boy. I still vividly remember our first encounter over dinner in Goa, where I was struck not just by his well-mannered demeanour but also by the spark of brilliance and kindness he exuded. Little did I know then that this same boy would one day embark on an incredible journey of transformation and self-discovery, ultimately culminating in a book that promises to inspire countless teenagers facing their own challenges. In my line of integrative medicine, I see teenagers almost every day, or young adults who were once teenagers, who faced the trauma of bullying. Many of them are healing, some are stuck, some are still victims of their trauma. Some have turned their struggles into strength. As a child, Amaan faced the painful trials of bullying, circumstances that could have easily crushed his spirit and confidence. However, instead of succumbing to despair, he took these experiences and channelled them into a powerful quest for personal growth. Through the establishment of meaningful routines, he found a sense of purpose that reignited his confidence and reshaped his life. It is this resilience and dedication that he shares with us in this book. "Road to Routines" is not just a narrative filled with the lessons learned from one young man's struggles, it is a beacon of hope and guidance for all teenagers navigating similar battles. In a world that often feels overwhelming, it emphasizes the transformative power of consistent habits and the importance of embracing routine to pave the way for dreams to be realized. I love the science and simplicity that Amaan has integrated together in this book to bring a simple yet powerful and doable read to everyone. I am huge believer that simplicity is the new luxury and it starts with what we learn and action. I want to remind all teens that Life may present you with suffering and struggles, but remember, every challenge is an opportunity for growth. Take all the help you need, express your emotions to trusted people and family, know that you are not alone and there is always help, and asking is a powerful virtue. We don't have to win big all the time, but we need to be consistent with solid habit, small wins and let that all accumulate into a powerful life story that you write for yourself. By harnessing the insights from this book, you will find that even the heaviest burdens can be transformed into strengths, leading you toward a brighter future. The power of routine. Congratulations to Amaan for not only overcoming adversity but for also courageously sharing this journey with the world with actions and ideas we can all implement. May your story uplift and inspire many, and continue to shine in this beautiful life you have created for you. I believe family and love are the most powerful drugs and I am honoured to know your parents and I truly appreciate them for being your healing drug through your journey.

With all my admiration,

luke coutinho

Luke Coutinho

Integrative and Lifestyle Medicine

Chapter 1

An Apple a Day Keeps the Doctor Away: The Power of Habits and Unveiling the Importance of Routines

The most powerful tool a man can possess is having the habit of implementing habits in their life. Habits help provide a specific type of structure in a person's life. They help clear the path filled with confusion and uncertainty, making it more transparent and visible.

Once upon a time, there was a boy who was your bare average boy. He loved sports, playing games, and spending time with his family. The only thing different about this boy was that his academic performance in school was below average, and even his social presence could have been better. However, this boy wasn't the type to give up, as most people in this failed generation do. This boy was different and knew his capabilities were less sharp than others. However, he also knew that he could still enhance his capabilities. He started looking for answers, browsing the Internet, reading books, and asking experts. After doing everything you could imagine, the boy learned a precious lesson at the end of this hunt. It wasn't his intelligence or mind holding him back. His poor style of living was the reason he was being held back. This boy had several imperfections, but he wasn't the type to not try to change his flaws and convert them into his strengths.

Habits

What are habits? Habits can be described in many different ways, depending on the person. Habits are not something that can make an individual successful instantly; instead, they are the tiny transformations people implement in their lives. Transformations that steadily set them up for success.

Even the most minor changes in our habits can help change the trajectory of our lives. The big misunderstanding about habits is that habits are activities that one does for only a day to help one transform one's life automatically. In the book Atomic Habits, James Clear mentions, "Success is the product of daily habits-not once-in-a-lifetime transformations". As mentioned earlier, habits can be life-changing only if implemented correctly.

This gives you an excellent, brief idea about habits as a general topic, but how do you get into the habit of implementing habits? To learn the art of implementing habits, one needs to know the 3-steps towards success, which will help them understand the right ways to implement habits, as well as help them learn how to get rid of habits that are not positive and instead slow down their productivity. These three steps include:

- Getting clear

- Simplifying and sticking

- Making it satisfying

Three Steps Towards Success

These three steps can help one add structure and clarity to one life and understand the key steps one can take to make implementing habits easier. One of the main reasons most people do not stick to habits is the lack of commitment. I used to face this in my early years of learning about productivity, and sometimes I still do.

Don't get me wrong; these steps will not magically get you to implement habits into your life. The main effort has to come from your end. "Strength and growth can only come through continuous effort and struggle," said Napoleon Hill. The three steps towards success is a revolutionary program, followed without compromise.

Getting Clear

Getting clear is the first step of the program. It is all about self-awareness, getting to know yourself better, reflecting and understanding, and **analyzing all your daily habits**. Everyone has habits, but that is not the goal of this chapter. The goal of this chapter is to turn all habits into positive habits rather than keeping the old, negative ones.

Once you understand the general habits you implement in your daily life, ensure you make a **list, categorizing them based on whether they are positive or negative.** This will help get rid of any uncertainty you have. Most people don't implement habits because of their lack of clarity. This is why this exercise is essential to get to know yourself better.

After you have categorized these, how do you slowly start **implementing those habits?**

A strategy that works best for me is **Setting deadlines.** This helps one maintain these habits. For most people, the 'starting of habits' is very hard. Therefore, deadlines help ensure that they complete their habits. I recommend setting these deadlines in terms of a **to-do list.**

Most to-do lists are very vague, and because of that, they do not serve their purpose, which is to help you perform tasks and stick to them; make them specific, and do not only state the topic you will be doing! I suggest mentioning the subtopic and the reason for your doing this. This will help you feel more accountable and increase your chances of actually doing the task. Don't forget to mention other factors, such as the environment you will be working/ studying in and if anyone else is learning with you, too.

Another efficient strategy James Clear mentioned in the book Atomic Habits: "**Stacking Habits**". Stacking Habits means using an already-built habit to help build another one by keeping it right after. This can be highly beneficial since it would help develop another habit with almost no effort since it uses an already existing habit.

All the points mentioned above were ways to implement new positive habits. However, what about negative ones? Studies suggest that people get attracted to things that are always present in their environment, so the answer is to simply remove all the unnecessary distractions from your study or workplace to ensure maximum productivity. Sometimes, the most confusing questions have the most straightforward answers. Here, **the only effective way to eliminate a bad habit is to remove it from your environment.**

Simplifying and Sticking

Humans are prone to do activities that we find attractive and fun. Some of our habits, even though they are essential, just do not appeal to our personal choices. Therefore, you need to make the habits more attractive so that you can perform them more often and stick to them. Making them simple is a very effective way to engage and stick with your habits. Most of us do not stick with our habits because starting a habit is one of the most complex factors when building habits. Therefore, when beginning to implement these habits, try to make them as simplified as possible. This will enable you to perform the habits with ease. Over time, you can then increase the difficulty levels of those habits.

Have you ever heard the quote, "Show me your friends, and I will show you your future?" As said by Dan Paye, this sentence is so much more than just a quote! It displays a critical point that people should realize: That one's life, the way they act, speak, and behave, revolves around the company they keep. This could benefit a person if they stick with the right influences.

Further, one of the best ways to create a link to those habits is keeping an **"Accountability Friend"**.

An accountability friend is someone who helps you stick to your habits. This plays a vital role in implementing habits since keeping a friend accountable can help increase the chances of sticking to your habits. Whenever I start anything new, my accountability friend is my mother. Why? Because she goes the extra mile and motivates me to complete the task ahead! One of the other ways to keep it more interesting is to keep a reward or a punishment. This can further increase productivity.

Another exciting way a person can stick to their habits is by **"Eliminating distractions"**. Studies suggest that humans are more prone to getting distracted when their environment consists of distractions. Now

I understand that as a human, I can't expect anyone to become fully isolated, away from distractions and humanity, solely focusing on their work. The world practically runs on the Internet, and being a part of it is imperative. One can implement some acute measures to help them stay focused, such as keeping all electronic devices in another room, hiding distracting items, etc. This can help make you 10x more productive and make it easier to implement your habits.

Making It Satisfying

This rule is all about rewarding yourself. This strategy is highly effective, and I recommend it to all my peers. As you may or may not know, this book focuses on the teenage audience. As a teenager, rewards are an essential part of our productivity journey since rewards and satisfaction can increase dopamine levels, which can be highly beneficial. Rewarding yourself is an advantageous strategy. Even the most minor reward, like chocolate or some me time for yourself, can do wonders for your overall mood and mental state.

Have you ever considered why bad habits are more favorable than good ones? This is because of a straightforward formula:

Bad habits = Immediate satisfaction but long-term disadvantages

Implementing good habits might be a difficult task, but it also leads to immense success:

Good habits = Not immediately pleasant but long-term advantages

A good and beneficial habit is challenging but can provide immense benefits once it is converted into your daily routine.

All of us have goals, right? Positive habits are a way of reaching them. "Give me six hours to chop down a tree, and I will spend the first four sharpening the axe," Albert Einstein famously says in this quote. There is a very evident correlation between the quote and the function of habits: **Habits are the axe that helps you achieve your goals.** The key takeaway from this section is this: The system of how you will reach your goal is as important, if not more important than, the goal itself. **Goals are temporary, and routines are forever.**

Importance of Routines

You might ask yourself, what is the next step Once habits have been implemented? After positive habits have been implemented, one has to stick to them for the habits to benefit them. This can sometimes be very challenging! Implementing habits is hard, but sticking to them is another level altogether. **Routines can help one structure their day, enabling them to stick to their positive habits and be as productive as they can throughout the day.** If you are a student reading this book, I understand the education system is complicated, and most of the time, you need more time to focus on other essential aspects of your life. All the great minds and the poorest procrastinators have one thing in common: the number of hours they have in a day.

No matter who you are or what your occupation is, we all only have 24 hours in a day, so it is crucial to spend our valuable time wisely on tasks and activities that will benefit and bring joy to our lives rather than procrastinating all day long and ending the day with having done absolutely nothing productive. This is the difference between **great people and procrastinators**. Great minds understand the importance of Time and learn how to prioritize it toward meaningful activities. On the other hand, procrastinators have no agenda and want to save valuable time that will never come back.

I often describe routines as the building blocks or pathways to success. Routines make implementing habits easier since they provide structure and a basic day outline. **Routines are used by great people worldwide,** but they will only be effective if you learn the correct way to use these routines and seamlessly implement them into your life.

Chapter 2

Decelerating the Clock:
Take Control of your Day and Time

An average adult makes about 35,000 decisions in a day! That might seem like a lot, but most people are used to making various daily choices. These decisions can impact or change the trajectory of their day. Decision-making is an important concept that most people should understand and incorporate into their lives. Many successful people who are widely known to have a lavish lifestyle, fast cars, and a lot of money often have some characteristics that they all share, one of which is understanding the importance of wise decision-making.

One can only do a certain amount of tasks in a day. **Prioritizing tasks** is a vital part of being successful. If you are a teenager in school, you will realize that you do not have time for every social gathering, every lecture, or every game night. One must understand that our time is limited, and nothing will last forever. I know that sounds depressing, but it is the truth. I am a teenager, and the only advantage I have over most of the best-selling authors in the world is 'time'. This Time can be a precious asset if it is used ideally. Even the deadliest weapon in the world, given to a child, is useless. It isn't in your favor unless you learn how to use Time.

The above example conveys that everything a person does needs to have **Intention.** Intention can be described in many ways, but intention is **What a significant individual will do to achieve their desired intention.**

Intentional Intention

Intention is about gaining clarity in the specific task you are trying to achieve. As a student, one will find themselves with several tasks to accomplish, and most of the time, it is only possible to perform some of the tasks at hand. This is where intention comes into play, **helping you prioritize critical tasks over insignificant ones.** Data suggest that the average person spends almost 7-8 hours a week just on decision-making when, in those 8 hours, they could be learning a new skill, trying to achieve a goal, or even catching up on the sleep hours they have lost. Once time is gone, it can never come back.

This is why working with intention is so important! Working on a task with intention provides structure to your life and helps eliminate the time-consuming act of decision-making. It is imperative to be conscious of your environment and situation. Most millionaires who own several significant companies have decisions and tasks thrown at them every second of the day. However, because they have excellent skills at decision-making and work with intention, they understand the depth of a task before acting upon it. This is the diagram that I use to prioritize tasks based on their importance.

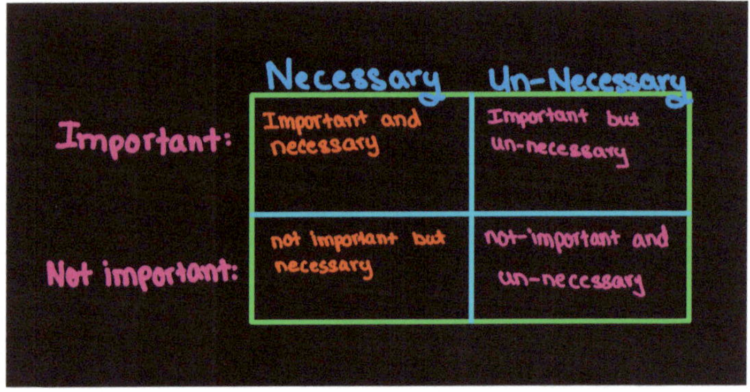

I would rather `understand two tasks well than do five without understanding them. Most people don't understand that **being 'busy' doesn't always mean 'better.'** I sometimes feel as though people feel that being busy is a good thing. However, do they ever think to themselves, 'Am I busy, or am I just doing this to get rid of the guilt of not doing much by focusing on tasks that are not important?'

Is Busy Better?

Everyone gets a sense of accomplishment after finishing multiple tasks, but do they ever reflect and ask themselves whether that task was really that important, or they just did it to stay occupied? Busy does not always mean better; this is the point most people need to understand. Rather than "acting busy," people could use this time to perform creative and joyful tasks. When people are busy, they feel like they have accomplished something. This might not always be the case, as you probably have realized by reading this paragraph.

Humans like to reward themselves to keep their emotions and moods high after they do something stressful or intense. In this world filled with the internet, social media, and electronic devices, one could not have had an easier way to get distracted. The internet world is so vast and creative that it sucks people into what I like to call the **"scrollathon"**. Don't get me wrong, social media is fantastic! It lets us stay in contact with our loved ones and know what is happening worldwide and many other things. Using the Internet and social media is not bad, but abusing it brings me to my next point.

Scrollathon

Scrollathon may sound confusing, but it is pretty simple. Its two words are joined together. "Scroll" refers to the constant consumption of media, and the word "action" is cut out from the word "marathon," which means running or traveling a long distance on foot. When these words are joined together, they become **Scrollathon**! I know you must be thinking, is this guy okay? The term is not that hard to understand, after all!

I did this because while you were reading what the word means, I wanted you to reflect as I carefully broke it down. I wanted you to realize how social media stops you from living more freely and intentionally. Most people let social media dictate their lives, which controls their emotions, moods, and perspectives, which is unhealthy! Returning to this chapter's first point, **I want to start living more 'intentionally'**!

An average person faces 60 distractions in a day, which is more than enough for you to slow down your productivity and not be able to reach your full potential. This is why it is essential to be aware of your surroundings and incoming distractions while knowing how to tackle them. Every day, I like to know how well or intentionally I have spent my time. For that, I use these simple **3-step, 3-minute highlights.**

1. Emergency

2. Satisfaction

3. Reward

1. Emergency

The first step towards gaining more awareness is to analyze the tasks at hand at the start of your day. If you are a student like me, you would have multiple assignments, homework, and tests due or coming up. At a point, it just gets overwhelming and can slow down your motivation. Therefore, the right way to do this is to start with the most critical or immediate tasks. I like to ask myself, **"What is the most important thing I need to do today,**

and how will it affect me in the future?" This specific question can help you clarify and define your objective for a particular task. The beauty of this question is that it allows one to reflect and understand the importance of time distribution throughout the day. It also helps us focus on the tasks and activities that matter over the ones that do not. Remember, this highlight is not to be taken lightly. One only needs to put down the most pressing and essential thing of the day, and if there are multiple tasks, one can put down even two. Anything more will not work since these emergency tasks require precision and focus. So, focusing on too many tasks that need to be completed in the emergency highlight might affect your productivity.

2. Satisfaction

Finishing your work, getting good grades, and focusing on assignments are essential, although something equally significant is rewarding and satisfying yourself. As humans, we need to understand that we are not machines. We can only be expected to work 24/7 without fatigue and focus loss. That's why short but meaningful breaks are essential for a person, so they understand there is more to life than just studies or work. Every human should feel like they have done something special today that may have uplifted their mood.

These tiny spikes in happiness can benefit long-term happiness. Everyone should enjoy the little things in life, and if you grant yourself a few minutes of satisfaction, it is perfectly fine and healthy. I ask myself for this highlight, **"What do I need at the end of today that would satisfy me?"** This question could be answered by reading a short novel you have been waiting to read or finally getting on a call with your significant other after a stressful day. The sole purpose of this highlight is to let go, relive, and extract yourself from all the stress you have been facing through the day.

3. Reward

This is the last and final highlight of the day and the most important one. The reward highlight is simple but also extremely important and influential. For this highlight, all you do is reward yourself! This reward can come in many forms. I am not asking you to buy a new Porsche because you finished your assignment, but instead a candy or an extra 5 minutes of screen time. I ask myself for this highlight, **"When I reflect on my day, what experience would give me the most joy?"** The most important advice I can give you from this chapter is that even the smallest of joys can significantly impact a person's mood.

When you group all these three categories into one, it helps you understand the structure of your day and dictates how the day will go. These three highlights can help change the course of your day. Once you have mastered identifying the tasks that go into these three highlights, there are further steps that you need to take to ensure their program runs smoothly.

Chapter 3

Lay the Groundwork: Establishing Routines to have a Path of Success

Most of the time, routines themselves can be described as a **pathway to success.** While routines are not the primary goal, **they are necessary for success.** In other words, routines are like the guiding light guiding you toward anything you want to achieve. This chapter is about setting up the essential groundwork for you to understand the critical components of **establishing routines.**

Remember that no one is perfect, and neither must they be so. Also, remember that routines are different for everyone. The point of a routine is for you to make your **personalized** agenda for the day. Remember that a routine adds 'structure' to your day. Therefore, it is a vital tool that can **make or break your day**. Before you implement any type of routine, you need to understand **'why' you need to implement it**. This is a vital step.

As said before, work is done better when done with intention! Therefore, determine your intention and why you want to implement these routines. This will help you understand your needs and wants and the changes that should be incorporated into your daily life to make implementing routines seamless.

Put it on paper.

The most effective way to understand what you do in a day while separating it into important and not-so-important tasks is by jotting it down! We cannot possibly work 24 hours a day because we must also focus on other 'essential' functions like eating and sleeping, which are equally important. Ensure you note what you do in all the additional hours of the day. That is the hours that are not part of those essential tasks.

To do list:
- ☐ Finish art assignment
- ☐ Workout
- ☐ Finish chem task
- ☐ Finish writting Chp 3
- ☐ Get a new book
- ☐ Finishing AI course

Breaking it down

After putting your daily tasks and activities on paper, we reach the next step, the most essential part. This is analyzing which tasks are important and those that are not. This step is vital because it is necessary to know what you should be spending more time on rather than procrastinating on tasks that are not necessary. Time is limited, and it is crucial to utilize it wisely! Breaking it down is effective. Also, an essential process is developing a routine that suits you and caters to your specific needs. Remember, don't let anyone else's thoughts affect you. Every human being has their perspective and opinions.

Tasks that may not be that important to them might seem extremely urgent to you. This routine will be personalized for you and your needs; therefore, try not to get intimidated and influenced by others' opinions and perspectives.

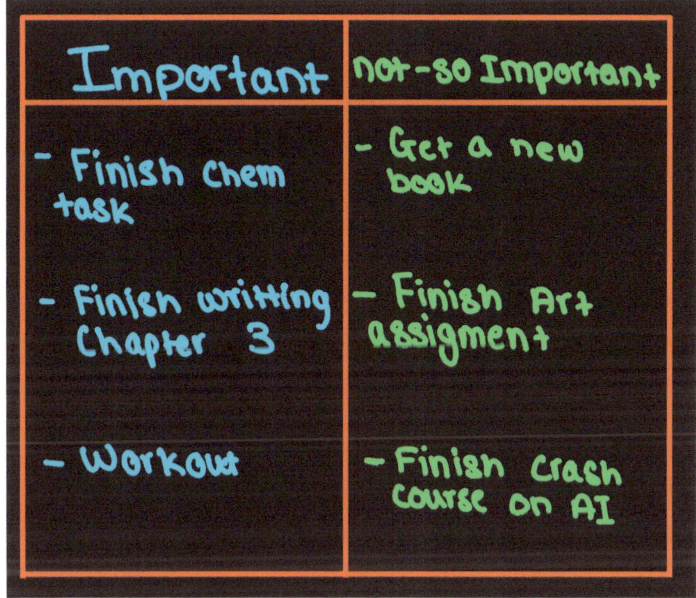

Finding the loopholes

The most challenging work is complete once you have passed the breaking-down phase! So, congrats to you! If you read this book, you are likely a student just like me, trying to sort out their life. The student faces tremendous pressure because of homework, expectations, extracurricular activities, etc. Finding time for other meaningful activities that might help one in the **long term is challenging.** A critical point I wanted to share with you before writing this book is that I always think long-term. I like to think of life as a marathon. Nobody wins the marathon by all-out sprinting! It might be efficient initially, but it will eventually cause fatigue and slow you down. However, if you strategically develop a plan to pace yourself through the marathon, the chances of you finishing it in a faster time would be higher than if you sprint. Coming back to my point, **a marathon depicts the race of life.** It cannot be won in a day. Instead, constant effort and strategic thinking will sooner or later get you there.

Therefore, focusing on the long-term aspect of any task will help you work on it more intentionally. However, what if you don't have time for these tasks? Well, the answer is straightforward: **Make time!** You might wonder how you would ever make time. Now, while you cannot extend a day's duration so that you can work on your desired tasks, you can certainly make time for these essential tasks by removing the unproductive and unnecessary tasks we do in a day. This is why the preceding step was so important. Breaking it down helped you realize how you spent your valuable time daily. Now that it has been done, I want you to do a straightforward task. I want you to observe what you have written and break it down.

Further, I want you to find any block of time in your day that you use to procrastinate and do unproductive things and change it into a **"Flow period".** We will understand flow periods later in this book, but for now, it means a work block, where you prioritize any task from your daily highlight and work on it. At first, things may start to slow, but you will eventually see the power of this tactic.

Trust me, it is extraordinary. Slowly but eventually, when you find more loopholes in your day, you will use them to your advantage to work on tasks that matter to you and help you long-term. At first, these will be called loopholes. Still, with your dedication, these become positive habits that effectively fit into your personalized routine and help you become productive.

Chapter 4

Beyond The Horizon:
The other Benefits that Routines
can help us Achieve

Until this chapter, I have been explaining how one can conduct routines and the several ways. But the most important thing I have not spoken about is how routines benefit us and help us achieve our most wanted goals in life. Our life is far too short to procrastinate and waste time on senseless activities.

Most people are scared of death, but I am scared of leaving this planet without doing anything significant or benefiting myself or society. I am just not the person who wants a usual 9-5 job and lives merely for the sake of living! Now, a standard job is satisfactory. You should do what you love most, but you should also not waste your life. Most people in this day and age are 'living but dead.' They have no hobbies or goals and are just trying to be **"average".** This, to me, is not acceptable. We humans are capable of doing so much more in life! We just need to try and reach that potential, but it's so hard to do that today because of the endless distractions in the world.

I would have laughed hysterically if you had told me three years ago that I would write a book about routines. However, here I am, doing just that! No human is perfect. Our lives are all about 'developing,' That is the beauty of life; we humans are continually developing and learning something new daily. Three years ago, I was a complete and utter mess. I hated school, I hated learning, I was lazy and agitated all the time, and I could never understand the reason for this until I discovered routines. The reason I was such a big procrastinator is that I never had any kind of structure to my day. I never had an agenda and worked without **intention**, which was the most significant fault I have ever made.

Are these routines actually that effective? My answer would be: It depends from person to person. Since I lacked clarity in my day and didn't have any purpose, routines helped me narrow things down and take strides toward working on my goals. It is beautiful if you are already very organized and working towards your goals without problems. However, adding structure and routines to your day will only make it better. This is why I am writing this book! **There are no downsides to routines.** All they do is make you a more productive person. Since I have been following these routines for quite some time, I want to share with you the ways I have developed as a student over the years by using productivity tactics while also working 'smarter' and not 'harder.'

Benefits of routines

A disclaimer that I want to present here is that seeing the magic of routines is subject to the amount of patience you possess. Though routines are very effective, it takes a little time to start seeing results. Though it comes slowly, it will surely come! So, all you need is faith and, of course, patience.

Ways routines can benefit

Once you have mastered the implementation of routines, there is physically and mentally nothing in your way to your path of success. While your personalized routine helps you get there, it also enables you to develop various other attributes that will benefit you in the long term.

A few skills that were very evident for me when I started practicing routines were:

Better self-discipline

Because routines are challenging to stick to in the beginning, since you have never tried anything like them, they require a lot of discipline. It might be hard at first, but you will start noticing that it gets easier as the days you implement those routines increase. This leads to you not even seeing that you are performing a routine one day. It has become part of your daily life. As this happens, you will be able to see how your self-discipline skills have improved since it is not an easy task and takes a lot of commitment and willpower.

Improved focus and concentration

When you start spending your time more wisely, rather than scrolling on social media sites, you try to learn a new, high-value skill. The whole point of routines is to remove all the bad habits and implement the good ones in your daily life. At the beginning of my journey, I was very restless. I could only focus for up to 15 minutes without easily getting distracted. After a while, though, every day when it was time for my 1 hour of learning a high-value skill, I learned ways to build concentration and improve my focus. I would have never done this if my routine structure hadn't been set up. Even though the courses I took about building concentration helped me, routines helped me channel my focus and concentration on the one particular task I was doing, which in this case was learning how to develop better focus and concentration.

Better time management skills

Routines are all about playing with time. Our time in a day is fixed, but there are endless possibilities of using this time. In this case, routines help one understand the importance of time management skills. When there are several tasks at hand, you can only complete them by managing the time you spend on each particular task. This means giving them equal importance, which only a routine can help. When you master how to use that limited time in a day well, you have acquired the most significant advantage anyone could have. Once you have reached the time management skill, nothing can stop you. This will help you use your time wisely for critical tasks rather than procrastinating over unnecessary things.

Life is so uncertain that one doesn't know what will happen. **Most people wait for the future to unveil itself correctly, but some control their future by controlling their circumstances.** What I mean by this is that no one is ever sure what will happen. **The only sure thing in life is uncertainty.** We might not be able to control our future, but we could mold it in our favor with the right decisions being taken in the present.

Routines play an essential role in molding the future! On a Sunday night, I religiously sit, jotting down all my tasks for the next day. I also write the layout of my day and how it will be. I cannot emphasize enough how much this helps. Knowing exactly what to do next is helpful to have everything written down for you. **An average human spends 7 hours a week contemplating the decisions they make.** Isn't that absurd? With all that wasted time and effort, there are countless other things a person could be doing. The stress and anxiety a person experiences while trying to make instantaneous decisions about work, school, and activities is immense. If all of this had been laid out the day before, so you would know precisely what you are doing every hour, it would save you so much time!

There are several benefits of following a routine. It's so simple yet so helpful! All you need to do is **start,** and then the rest will take care of itself.

Chapter 5

Revolutionizing Routines: Making a Modern Guide on How to Build a Routine

I hope you are as excited to learn routines as I am about to teach you about building your personalized routine. Making your routine is a challenging part. The hard part is 'adapting' to it. You need to understand that your routine will change over time, and you must make a few small and significant changes as you advance into new chapters of your life. I will be explaining to you the steps to build a routine in an unorthodox way, but trust me, it's going to be helpful.

Think of yourself as a seed; you are nowhere near a plant. To become a healthy plant, what are the necessary precautions and steps you take to thrive in your ecosystem? These steps of 'seed-building' can be like building a routine. Once these steps have been conquered, you are pretty much done and will thrive in your 'ecosystem.'

The steps towards building your personalized routine are as follows:

1. Choosing the right plant

2. Selecting the environment

3. Getting to know its needs to be healthy

4. Catering to its needs

5. Maintaining and providing ongoing care

Choosing the right plant

This is the first step towards building your routine! When we choose a plant for ourselves, what factors do we consider? There are a few essential questions that I would ask myself before buying a plant. Firstly, you need to understand the **purpose** of this plant and why you need it. Secondly, you need to ask yourself how this will **impact** your life.

The impact doesn't have to be huge; it can even be small. The last question you must ask yourself is, **what other factors must I consider while buying this plant?** Mind you, this question is a little tricky! It makes you think that buying the plant isn't the only factor. Watering, nourishing, and contracting soil are also crucial factors.

How is this related to building my personalized routine? Well, all of the questions you would ask yourself when buying a plant are directly related to the questions you would ask yourself when getting into the habit of routines. Questions that make you reflect on facts like **Purpose, impact, and external responsibilities.** These help you understand how your routine is going to be. Understanding these key points will help you clarify your purpose and reinforce why you wanted to start your path to a routine in the first place.

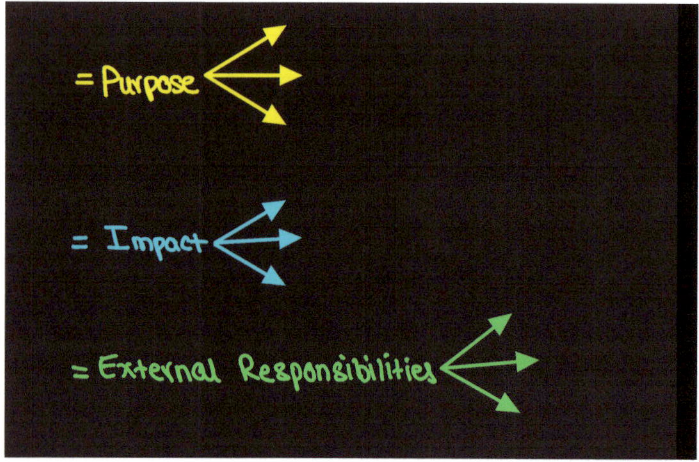

Selecting the environment

After you have purchased your plant, it is time to find the perfect environment. You scavenge and see various places where you could put this plant, but ultimately, you must choose the most optimal location for your plant. This is only because you want it to thrive and get substantial sunlight so it can grow beautifully.

After understanding the purpose, impact, etc. of implementing routines, you must start by reflecting on your day. Try to know how your day plays out. For the next couple of days, I want you to take a piece of paper and write down everything you do from morning to night. This must include study sessions, school/work, and all possible activities.

Once this has been done, you need to understand which environment you work best in. Our brain likes to be familiar with things, which means it wants to be familiar with the events throughout your day. Now, most events in this world are impromptu, although there are some that you are set to do every day, like studying, eating, and sleeping. Therefore, having designated spots for certain activities can help improve focus and concentration when immersed in our routines. It's a way to subconsciously tell our brain it's time to work. Surprisingly, it works very well! Now, remember the spot you chose should only be used when focusing on the task that requires that spot. It will be ineffective if other distractions are allowed and used in this space, although if your confined to a specific location, make sure to remove all the distractions that might leave you astray from your task.

I have kept a designated spot for writing my book. I like sitting by my window, hearing the sounds of Nature, and looking at the trees while I work. This place is so special for me. It's a haven where I can peacefully focus on my tasks without distractions.

After selecting the environment marked off the list, we move on to understanding this plant's needs. In other words, it means understanding the things necessary for this plant to live a good life and not have any difficulties. While you are getting to know the needs of this plant, you need two vital attributes: **Intention and Attention.** You will be successful only if you intend to determine and pay attention to your daily needs and have an intention for the day.

When you start a routine, you must understand the tasks you will do over your day. Functions that will keep you productive and fulfill your desired needs for the day. Even before you start your routine, you need to pay close attention and understand what those things are that you spend time on daily. Be they productive or unproductive, you need to know whether **you need them.** You might tell me, Amaan, there are so many things I do not need but are yet part of my daily life and routine, which is okay! All you have to do is replace the 'bad' wants with the 'good' ones.

No matter what is happening throughout your day and life, there are some non-negotiables that you have to stick to, which are also part of your routine. Your **non-negotiables** cannot be avoided at all costs and must be done no matter the circumstances. Remember, nobody becomes great without their fair share of sacrifices. Your non-negotiables aim to make you a better follower of routines and help you enjoy the process.

Non-negotiables are the few activities that you do daily that help you stay **energized and productive** throughout the day. Moreover, they can also be seen as a milestone you have finished in a certain amount of time or section of your day. Thus, I am ending the day with some positive action.

Catering to its needs

Once the needs have been set, and you know how to take care of them, it's time to cater to them. What I mean by 'catering to your needs' is spending the next few days trying out these non-negotiables and seeing how they work for you. The idea is to try setting up fixed timings for when you practice these activities.

I am not going to beat around the bush here. The first few days of implementing something completely new in your life are challenging and stressful. However, if you are reading this and have been dedicated to getting so far in the book, you are also committing to implementing these new habits!

Things can change after the plant gets its necessary needs over time. Its needs may grow. In this case, you need to cater to whatever your plant needs, staying persistent in modifying its needs based on the situation.

The same goes for you. Your non-negotiable needs can be modified and changed over time to fit your specific needs and help you acquire the state of maximum productivity.

Maintaining and providing ongoing care

I am thrilled to inform you that this will be the easiest step in this process! Now that the plant has gotten everything it needs, all it has to do is grow beautifully, turning into something marvelous. As time passes, you only need to make minor changes in its environment to fit best and suit the plant's needs.

The same goes for you! Now the hard work is finished, it is time for you to unleash the Productivity Beast in you, focusing and prioritizing your needs over everything, enabling you to grow beautifully, too.

Chapter 6

Two Turns to Innovation:
How to be Creative and Productive
Throughout the Day

Have you felt ready to work and be productive throughout the day? The first few hours have gone by quickly because of your effectiveness. But then suddenly, you feel tired! The surge of learning and working has disappeared. Many people face this problem and need help understanding how to tackle it. I call this the "**Productivity curve**". The productivity curve is a graphical representation of how well or how productive you stay throughout the day. Now, this representation is not the same for everyone. Some people are better off working longer hours at a stretch, while others work the same amount but in bits.

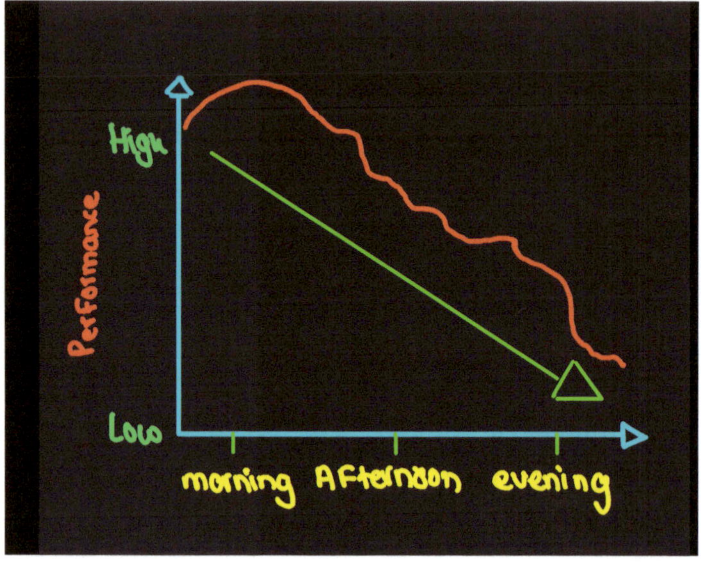

No matter how or where you work, in this day and age, there are several distractions that every human being faces. One needs to understand how to get past these distractions. Before going any further, it is essential to answer the following questions. I want you to keep all the answers written on a page somewhere that we will return to later. Further, these are the prompts that you need to answer, which will give you a generous amount of time to reflect on the following questions:

Understand when and where you work best

Timings and reasons for productivity increase and decrease

Optimum sleeping and waking up time

Parts of the day when you struggle with tasks

Understanding where you would like to allocate your valuable time

An average human brain has 70 thousand thoughts in a day. As I have said multiple times in this book, being productive and creative is challenging because of our daily distractions. That being said, I do have a solution for this. Remember, everything in this book boils down to intention and reflection. You need to ask yourself questions, as if you were asking another person, and figure out the answer. Further, when the Reflection and Intention have been done, you must incorporate the solution into your life routine.

Mental Playground

Mental Playground - this term is very self-explanatory. Your mental state is filled with overwhelming thoughts, which come and exit from your attention like a playground filled with children doing one activity and then moving on to the next. Our mental playground is composed of the thoughts and feelings we are aware of in the current moment, and most times, it can get extremely overwhelming. Constantly catering to these thoughts prevents you from being productive and creative. This is because you can only focus on one thought or task.

It is essential to know what is going on in your mental playground. 70% of the information going through involves unnecessary thoughts. Thoughts that are important but not in the present moment. I can classify these thoughts into **essential** and **unimportant** **using this simple diagram**.

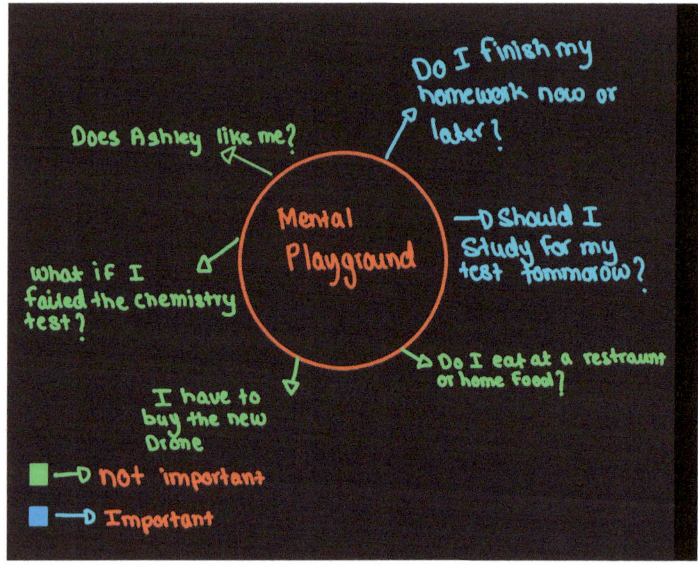

Using this diagram, you can easily understand which thoughts are important and need to be attended to and which are unnecessary and can be dealt with later. "The only impossible journey is the one you never begin"- Tony Robbins. **We all have so much potential in life, but none will be possible without action**. You must wonder what I do now that I have distinguished my mental playground's tasks. Most people do nothing, but you will! You will use the most essential functions in your mental playground to structure your day. You must reflect and identify how many "mental playground tasks" you can complete. Then, simply spread them out throughout the day; I like to call these "Brushing blocks," where I brush off the task from my mind into something physical.

You have yet to learn how much stress this releases. You will instantly feel lighter in your mind. Most of us don't appreciate or enjoy our time on this planet. Well, you should, because it's constrained! Every day, all people are doing is just worrying and being held up by the unnecessary thoughts that are going on in their minds. They don't get to enjoy anything around them, which is truly sad. Therefore, with some practice, you can choose what you want to put in your mental playground, which will benefit you in the long run. Once again, our attention on our tasks should be with Intention. Most people get into an "autopilot mode," making them do tasks like zombies without focus and outcome. This is the foremost thing that can lead to decreased productivity.

So, you need to keep checking on your mental playground. That will keep you in check, ensuring you stay 'on task' and don't deviate from your goals and aspirations. If one acquires this vital skill, they will eventually build discipline, which will benefit them not only in the short term but also in the long term!

A book I read a few years back, Hyperfocus by James Bailey, spoke about focusing on one task at a time and how you become more engrossed in your work and enter the "flow state". This flow state is genuinely magical. It's a state you get into while focusing on a particular task. You are so focused that you lose track of time and are completely immersed in what you're doing.

Flow state

Flow state is a potent practice if used correctly. The first time you enter a flow state will be magical! It's so powerful that you won't even know you were in a state of flow until you are out of it. Yes, it's that powerful. But how do you get into this state of flow? **Follow these steps to try and enter a block of flow state:**

Focus on your mental playground, and analyze the most critical task needing attention.

Look at your routine (once it has been made) and find a block in which you could prioritize the practice of flow state.

Commit to doing it at that specific time.

Eliminate all types of external distractions and have the agenda cleared.

Work diligently for an hour or an hour and a half.

You can enter the flow state if these practices are followed. This will be revolutionary. It's an essential part of your routine. At first, you can only have one block of flow state in your routine. This is because the real battle is before the flow state. You must ensure that nothing is in your mind, only the task. **"Do not dwell in the past, do not dream of the future, concentrate the mind on the present moment"- Buddha.** The future is important, but for entering the flow state, you only need to **focus on the present**. You should not do more than one flow state in a day because often, a flow state drains your energy since you have given your hundred percent in that hour or hour and a half.

This is a good thing. It shows that your body can focus for only a certain amount of time, after which your productivity curve falls. A long-distance runner doesn't start with a 100km race when he is a beginner but instead does short bursts of 5 km to **build** his stamina and endurance until he can finally compete in a 100km race. Although this is very challenging, it can be done. The same goes for the time we spend in the flow state. At first, it is difficult to focus for more than an hour since it is mentally exhausting. But as time passes, you will get better and can concentrate for extended periods without being quickly exhausted and distracted.

The whole point of this chapter is for you to understand how to unleash the maximum productivity and creativity you can have. The answer is, engaging in flow states, enabling you to work efficiently and get shit done!

Chapter 7

Structural Shapers:
How one's Regime Revolves around "See" (Sleep, Eating, Exercising)

These four aspects, which I call the Structural Shapers, are like the pillars of productivity in your life. If followed to the tee, it can revolutionize your entire life! When you learn a language (I am learning French), even though it might be beautiful, it comes with challenges. For learning any language with a certain amount of ease, it is essential to learn and master a few fundamentals that will help and guide you.

The same goes for you when you are just implementing your routines. You need to learn and understand the fundamentals, even though they are apparent. Deep diving into them and understanding their implications is a potent skill you will obtain that will eventually benefit you. The information in this book is robust. It has significantly changed my life, and it can change yours, too. That is, as long as you try and follow these steps to the best of your ability.

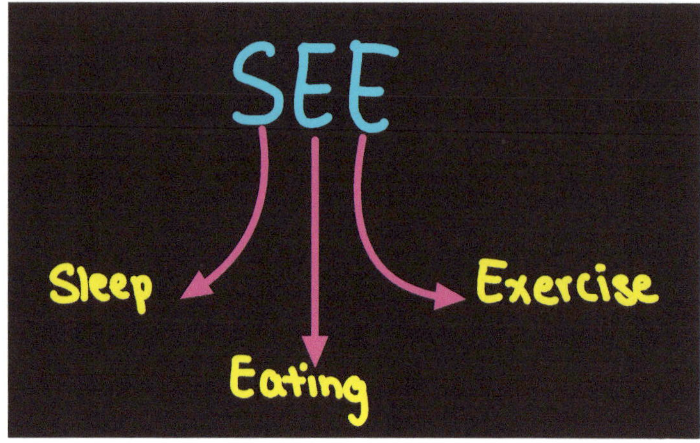

Sleep

Sleep is essential to anyone's life, whether a nerd or an athlete. It plays a vital role in everyone's life. If our sleep schedule is inadequate, it can lead to severe disadvantages and issues, which we will cover later. After a long day of work or school, you come home and feel like it's time to rest and sleep. The funny thing about this is that most people think that when we sleep, our body shuts off. But that is incorrect; while sleeping, our body plays a vital role in repairing and maintaining our bodily functions. During sleep, the body repairs metabolic faults, glucose generation, and cardiovascular problems.

It nurses our bodies overnight for us to wake up in optimum condition the next day. This is why sleep is the most critical factor in my routine and should be in yours, too. If you have not noticed, our sleep directly impacts anything we do. For instance, when studying for an exam, if we haven't gotten adequate sleep, our bodies will not be able to perform well. For example, if we are trying to learn a new skill, and if we have not gotten a good quality of sleep the previous night, our body will not be able to register things as fast as it usually can.

Think of it as an electronic item. When we have put it on charge (sleep in this context), it is charging for the next day, and when we remove it, it is on 100% (when we have just woken up). Later in the day, the battery keeps decreasing until, when you are back at home, it is 20% (after being active for hours, our body gets tired). Then, we put it on charge again for the next day!

In another scenario, what if your charger doesn't work well? In the morning, your phone is only 40% (meaning you will be able to work but will not be at optimum performance), and after half the day, the phone is dead (your bodily functions are at risk because you haven't gotten good sleep, and now can't be productive).

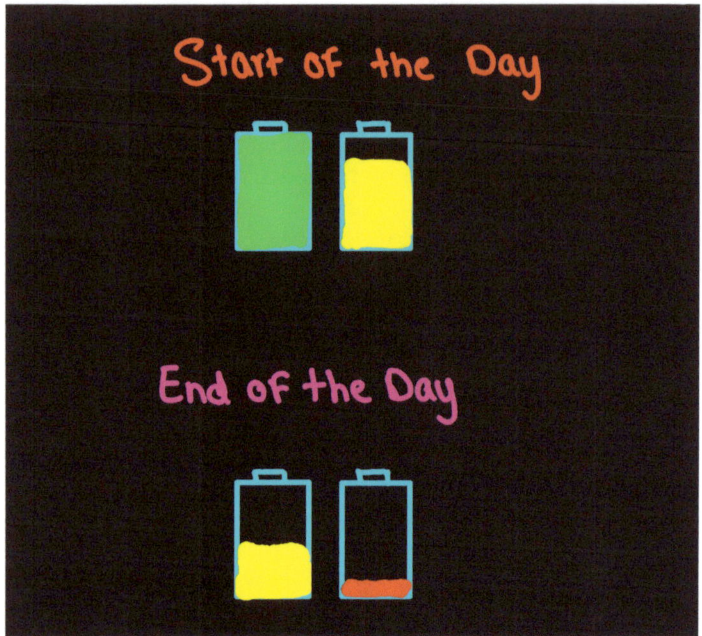

Are you getting the point? If you haven't been able to rest well and charge yourself up, you will not be able to perform throughout the day, will slowly but surely give up, and will want to relax. In simple terms, sleep is highly underrated! The better the sleep, the better the performance in your exhausting daily activities. Not only the amount of sleep but even the quality of the sleep matters greatly. Sleep is responsible for many of our daily functions; I think now is the time to delve into the exciting and profound world of **"sleep cycles"**.

Sleep cycles are patterns that are recurring. These patterns enable us to have sleep stages we go through every night while sleeping. Typically, there are **four stages of sleep.** We go through each of these stages in our sleep cycle. **Stage 1** is light sleep, transitioning from being awake to slightly sleeping. This stage is the shortest since it only takes a few minutes. **Stage 2** is when you go into a little more profound sleep. The few indicators that tell you are in stage 2 are a decreased heart rate or a lower body temperature. Furthermore, when moving on to **stages 3 and 4,** we have entered deep sleep, in which our body repairs all our tissues and muscles, builds energy for the next day, boosts our immune system, and checks other vital processes.

By now, you see the actual importance of sleep. Even though you are resting, your body is more active than ever; working on so many processes ensures you are **one hundred percent** when you wake up. When these sleep cycles have not been completed, your body is not fully recharged and up to the mark. **I can compromise on anything and everything, but not my sleep.**

If your sleep cycle is not up to the mark, no worries! Here are a few strategies that I used to get my body to its hundred percent while sleeping:

1. **Limiting exposure to screens:** Most moms tell us that our phones are the cause anytime we are sick or not performing well. I hate to say it, but that's true regarding our sleep! Most phones emit blue light that interferes with our sleep cycle and quality. So, try avoiding using your phone at least an hour before sleep.

2. **Controlling your environment:** I am sure you have learned through this book that our environment plays a significant role in everything we do, including sleep. I have understood that even the slightest light in my room can affect my sleep. So, if you are not scared of the dark like me, keep your bedroom as dark as possible while sleeping. If you do this, you will start seeing changes the very night you do this, getting a better sleep.

3. **Creating a bedtime routine**: Creating a bedtime routine is very efficient. Once you get the hang

of it and do it regularly, it is like a signal to your body that says, "Okay, it is now time to sleep!" It helps you finish your stage 1 faster and gives you the right **quality** and **quantity** of sleep.

Eating

Consumption of food is one of the most important factors of living. An average person spends **32,098 hours** of their lifetime eating. Isn't that wild? If an average person spends so much valuable time eating food, they should eat the right amount and ingredients to keep themselves healthy and fit. The ingredients we consume are vital for significant amounts of biological processes to occur, such as **blood sugar regulation, energy levels, nutrient supply to the brain, and digestive health.** These are only a few factors our eating is responsible for. Therefore, maintaining a healthy diet is crucial and could be helpful in the long term. There are a few steps that you can follow that will enable you to eat the **right amount** of the **right food**.

1. Limit processed foods: Nowadays, more processed foods are worldwide than natural ingredients. This is because people would instead

enjoy 'artificial' tastes of food. While this is not necessarily bad, it is essential to have processed foods in limited quantities and make sure you are not over-consuming them.

2. Meal timing: Meal time is the most underrated strategy. When you have constant timings of activities such as eating and sleeping, it can help your body regulate its processes optimally.

3. Staying hydrated: Drinking a good amount of water is essential, as when you hydrate your body, it performs better than it usually does. Water also helps benefit from many more things, like flushing out toxins from our bodies.

Exercise

Let me clarify: you are not perfect in any way, and neither am I! A great example of this would be **exercise**. I love eating food and despise working out. At first, I used to look down upon exercise, thinking it was all about getting my abs to look more muscular. I started to exercise at first two times a week, then moved on to 3 times a week, and now I exercise 4 times a week. I see changes not only in my body but also in my mental well-being and productivity.

I realized exercise is more than just 'looking fit.' It caters to so many other vital factors of your life. Knowing this has changed my perspective on exercising and being fit. Here are a few ways exercising helped me with my overall health and productivity:

1. Physical traits: When you work for a significant amount of time and get a reward, there is no better feeling. Similarly, when you exercise and are committed to a strict diet, nothing can stop you from achieving your physical goals. When talking about 'physical,' I don't mean looking good. Exercise helps with biological processes being conducted in your body, too. Such as assisting in making our muscles and bones more substantial and even helping with our cardiovascular health.

2. Better sleep: Everything is connected in some way or the other. Regular exercise can help benefit your sleep quality and make you feel more energized after waking up the next day.

3. Improved mental health: Poor mental health is something I used to suffer from on and off in my life. It's not that anything was missing, but rather, some early life traumas I experienced left a scar on me. Life is not always going to be flowers and butterflies! Sometimes, there will be downs, but I have learned that the **bigger the fall, the better the rise.** Personally, it has helped me better my mood anxiety and put my energy in a positive direction.

Chapter 8

The Morning Momentum &
The Evening Elegance: The two most
Important Times of Your Day

Our day revolves around two main aspects: the **morning** and the **evening**. You might wonder why. I have a straightforward analogy explaining why these two periods are essential. When we wake up, it is the time our body has just been recharged and is ready to go. Thus, we are at our optimal state in the morning. After your stressful and tiring day, when it's time to recharge, you sleep, which is essential and part of your evening routine. This can also be the opposite. If you are a night owl, you charge up in the night and are sleepy and tired in the morning!

Most people need to learn which column they fit under. You need to take the following tests that will help you determine what time you are at your best state:

1. Try to learn a different skill for two days.

2. Try to understand and learn the first skill in the morning between 5 and 6 a.m.

3. The next day, try to learn another skill in the night between 10 and 11 pm.

4. After 4-5 days, do an oral and physical quiz and check which skill you have retained better.

After conducting this test, analyze which one had better retention. The one with the better retention rate will also be the one you focus more on. This enables you to understand which period your body works best in. No matter what time of the day you are at your optimal state, you must give equal importance to both routines. It's like a seesaw. For it to be balanced, both factors must be balanced, or the magical effect of routines will not occur. In our ever-so-busy schedule, we find it very hard to give time to other essential things that matter. If that was the case, now it should not be. The most significant use of time is the morning and evening for doing something you love, catching up on work, or learning a skill.

Your work timings determine whether you are an early bird or a night owl. We only have 14-15 hours in which we are not sleeping and are doing work. Our school and office occupy more than half of that time, leaving us only 1-2 hours to spend 'flowing' and doing quality work. You must be wondering why we don't just choose one time of the day. Why do we need to have a morning and afternoon routine? I have names for both these times of the day. The part of the day where I work best is called the "**energy block**". This is because I work best now and am charged up. In the afternoon, I am in my "**recharge block**". Let's understand what these times of the day mean in detail.

Energy block

The energy block in your day is the most important and influential time. It's hard to describe in words the power of the energy block. It's when you are focused and immersed in your work. Though energy blocks are very effective, you must learn how to use them wisely. Though these help you increase your productivity, they can also tire you out relatively quickly. With the exercise shown above, you can genuinely understand your optimal time of doing work and being productive. Using this knowledge, you can integrate energy blocks within your routine and stay consistent until they become second nature.

One of the most essential factors while conducting your energy block is the **placement of it** in your routine. From personal experience, because I am an early bird, I like to incorporate my energy blocks early in the morning since I work best and my mind is clear. Your energy blocks can be used for any activity as long as it is productive. I use them to catch up with schoolwork since I could be a better pupil. However, at other times, I use them to learn trading analysis, drop shipping, freelance editing, and various other activities. My only rule that you should follow, too, is that **it has to be productive**.

I give so much importance to energy blocks because they are the only time I can enjoy myself and work on something I love. This world is filled with endless distractions, and the only time I can escape from all that is by fully immersing myself and focusing on my tasks. Though we are working in this energy block, it feels like an escape from reality. It is truly magical once you try it. The flow state and the energy block are related since the energy block is the direction you must go to achieve the flow state.

Recharge block

A big misconception most people have is that the energy block is more important than the recharge block. Let's say you are in a race and have a sports car. The sports car enables you to go fast and potentially win the race if you are good (Sports car: Energy block), but if you forget to add fuel to your race car, it will be unreliable and stop eventually (Fuel: Recharge block). Although winning the race is essential, ensuring you have completed all the preparations is vital. "By failing to prepare, you're preparing to fail". -Benjamin Franklin.

Preparation is as necessary as the action. The sooner you release and implement that, the better. Our recharge block is like a preparation block. It helps us prepare for the next day. Since I am a morning person, I use my recharge blocks efficiently and wisely. After a long day of studying and school, my recharge block is mainly to have fun and prepare for the next day. Refrain from getting the wrong impression; I am not asking you to utilize every moment of your life toward development. Sometimes, it's just lovely to sit back and relax. Sometimes, doing **very little** is a **lot**. The recharge block is pretty simple. According to me, all you do is **recharge.**

I like to divide my energy block into three crucial parts.

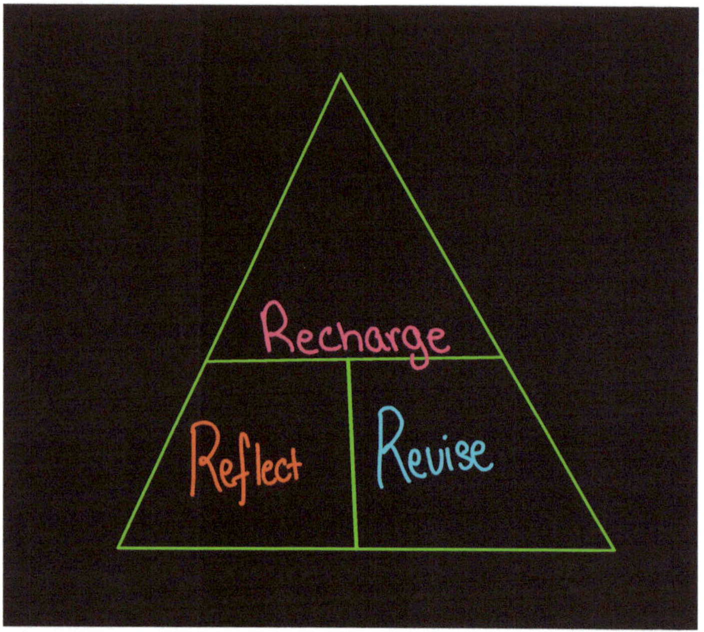

Recharge

This first one is self-explanatory. All you do here is recharge! You could do anything except work. You could watch TV, chat with your friends, or even sit idly and do nothing **as long as it brings you joy and happiness.**

Reflect

Over the years, I used to journal on and off. Journaling is something that I have always found to be very powerful.

However, for most people and me, it is something that you need to commit to. As we all know, commitment is scary in any context. However, once you start getting the hang of it, journaling helps you understand your day and evening. Too. It helps give you clarity on a lot of stuff. If you are thinking of journaling, do it using a pen and paper. Now, it is a digital world. Where am I going to have time for that? If you promise me you will journal regularly, I can offer an incentive for you. My email will be located at the end of the book. I will send you all a free journal for a few lucky human beings, so feel free to email me! Anyway, coming back to the point, I don't want to spoil anything. Try it out for 15 days religiously, and you **will** see a change!

Revise

Revise is the last and final step of your recharge block, in which you need to plan for the next day. Most of the time, we are too lazy to do tasks because we need more clarity. This can be solved by planning almost everything a day before so that you don't need to waste time and just get right to it. At the end of the book, I will give my format of noting things down the next day for the revised section of the recharge block.

Chapter 9

The Next Chapter:
How to Sustain and add Changes to your Routine

Sometimes, most people don't give themselves credit when it's due. I want you to give yourself a pat on the back. Most people want to improve their life, but they are too lazy. I can assure you that you are not one of them. If you have ever doubted yourself, thinking you are not consistent or productive, your reading this is a sign that anything is possible! At the start of the book, I am sure some of you would have thought, "How will I complete this book?" or "Can I even complete it?" And look at you now, almost at the finish line!

One misconception I want to help clear is that no **routine is perfect, nor will any routine ever be perfect.** As humans, we evolve daily. This includes our mental and physical traits; as these traits keep changing, so does your routine. Your routine might change once in 10 years or once in two months; it is okay to have a routine that benefits you. I am writing this book for you to follow only some of what I have said and apply it in your life. Even 'I' don't do that, being an author myself! Even if you change one small thing, that would mean the world to me. So, do not take it too seriously. Our routines, habits, likes, character, and more will keep changing. Only one thing should never change: being a kind and good person. Believe it or not, I see potential in every one of you reading this book; whether you are 50 or 15, trying to make a positive change in your life is commendable.

Returning to what I said, your routine truly and solely depends on your needs and wants. There is no such thing as a **bad** or **good** routine. The only way to understand whether your routine needs change is by self-reflection. As I have mentioned, Journaling is a powerful tool that helps us realize many things we don't normally do. I recommend you do this sparingly. Once in 1-2 months would be adequate since it would give you substantial time to reflect. Then, you could see if you needed to take action when it comes to changing your habits and routines.

Remember, it is unnecessary to change your routines every two months. I have been following the same routine for over eight months and have only made a few minor tweaks here and there. Otherwise, this has been my routine for quite a long time. Returning to some of the points in the earlier chapters, remember the journey to reach the destination of completing the same routine for eight months. I used to be very inconsistent regarding religiously following my routines, but as I said before, time heals and makes everything fall into place. I would have never thought that Amaan, who has anxiety and trauma from his childhood, would be writing a book. Nor would I have believed that Amaan, whose mom had to force him to do work, would fall in love with learning and productivity. **You will never be the same person you were in the past**, and the beauty of humans is that we are constantly evolving.

Though following routines and being productive throughout the day is a magical journey, it sure comes with its ups and downs, so make sure to have fun and enjoy the process and structure of your day.

Chapter 10

The Final Step: An Accumulation of Everything you have Learned

That's it, ladies and gentlemen, and we have reached the last and final stage, which is accumulating everything I have taught you so far into a routine. The following is an example of how you can create your routine! This helps you get inspiration to make your own. This routine will be constructed in 3 parts:

1. The day before the routine

2. The routine

3. End of the routine

The day before the routine

I advise people to do many different things at night before they start their day. This would give that day more structure and make it easier for the person.

- To-do list: Making the to-do list a day before is highly recommended by most productivity enthusiasts since it gives you an idea of how your day will look. Afterward, you could use the strategies in this book, such as putting tasks on paper and finding loopholes.

- Flow state/ Work block: Work blocks are mighty if used correctly. Therefore, figuring out when and where you will initiate your work block would be very helpful.

- Priority list: Besides making a to-do list, it would also be helpful if you made a more **specific** list, which will help you understand the most critical task and the task that can be completed later.

The routine

The routine is when all the work you thought about in "The Day Before the Routine" comes into action. It is time to finish all the tasks set for you throughout the day.

- Choosing the environment: Choosing the environment is a very underrated skill. Having a dedicated environment to do work can help you focus and have fewer things to worry about.

- Mental playground: Frequent checks on your mental playground help you understand what is going on in your mind, after which you could acknowledge those thoughts and then act upon them later. Focusing on the present task is what matters most.

- Placing your recharge and energy block: I recommend having a fixed time for this, but because our lives are filled with impromptu decisions, simply having 1 of these blocks is essential for us to have a positive and productive day ahead.

Ending the routine

Ending your routine well is as important as starting it. Following a few things will help you prepare for the next day and live more intentionally.

- Journaling: Journaling is a potent tool many people look down upon. The impact it has had on me is tremendous.

- Intentional reflection: Though intentional reflection comes under journaling, sitting down every minute or two, just thinking about how your day went, whether there were a few ups or downs, can help you understand yourself better and help you make better decisions in the future.

This is the complete guide to initiating and sustaining a routine in your life, to make your life more productive and structured; though this is the end of the book, I hope the teachings stick with you forever. Writing this book has been a joy, and I hope you are set on a path of prosperity.

www.ingramcontent.com/pod-product-compliance
Lightning Source LLC
Chambersburg PA
CBHW040913110726
48005CB00006B/874